Citizen Dog

by Mark O'Hare

**Andrews McMeel
Publishing**

Kansas City

Citizen Dog is distributed by Universal Press Syndicate.

Citizen Dog © 1998 by Mark O'Hare. All rights reserved. Printed in the United States of America. No part of this book may be used or reproduced in any manner whatsoever without written permission except in the case of reprints in the context of reviews. For information write Andrews McMeel Publishing, an Andrews McMeel Universal company, 4520 Main Street, Kansas City, Missouri 64111.

98 99 00 01 02 BAH 10 9 8 7 6 5 4 3 2

ISBN: 0-8362-5186-5

Library of Congress Catalog Card Number: 97-74515

Cover illustration by Nick Jennings

www.uexpress.com.

For Julie

Foreword

by Kevin Fagan

I laughed so hard at **Citizen Dog** one day that I actually got the hiccups. It's true! To get rid of them, I had to drink water through a straw while plugging my ears and holding my nose. I don't know where that remedy came from originally, but my grandma taught it to me, and now I'm passing it along to my fellow **Citizen Dog** fans. We may need it from time to time!

From the moment I saw **Citizen Dog**, I loved it. In case the strip is brand new to you, it's the story of a man and his dog. Or maybe it's the other way around. I haven't quite figured out which one is in charge. All I know is, Mel and Fergus are a great comedy team. Their relationship is kind of hard to explain, though. Let's just say it's more complicated than normal.

Mark O'Hare has a wonderful drawing style to go along with his amazing cleverness. His work never fails to brighten the day a little. **Citizen Dog** is new on the scene. But after reading this book, you may feel like it's been part of your life forever. I have a hunch that it will be.

— Kevin Fagan,
creator of **Drabble**

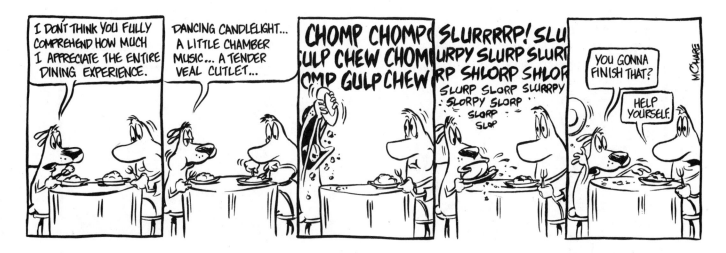

13

18

22

24

28

DOGS CAN PICK UP A VARIETY OF BAD HABITS.

TO RE-ESTABLISH CONTROL, IT IS IMPERATIVE THAT YOU DISCOVER THE SOURCE OF HIS NEGATIVE BEHAVIOR.

IF HE'S MADE IT TO CHAPTER FIVE, IT MAY BE TOO LATE.

IF HE WON'T OBEY, TRY REASONING WITH HIM. | YOU MUST BE FIRM AT ALL TIMES.

REMEMBER, A LITTLE DIPLOMACY CAN GO A LONG WAY. | LOOK HIM STRAIGHT IN THE EYE AND TELL IT LIKE IT IS.

WILL YOU **PLEASE** STOP CHEWING THE DRAPES.

NO.

HE MAY BE BELLIGERENT. KEEP TRYING! | HE'LL TRY THE DIPLOMACY ANGLE. DON'T GO FOR IT.

YOU MIGHT WANT TO CONSIDER OPENING UP MORE TO YOUR HOUSEMATE.

LETTING DOWN YOUR WALL AND ADMITTING A PARTICULAR FAULT OF YOUR OWN IS ALWAYS A GOOD START.

I'VE BEEN A LITTLE TOO IMPATIENT WITH YOU. | I'VE BEEN USING YOUR TOOTHBRUSH.

IT'S AMAZING WHAT A DIFFERENCE A LITTLE COMMUNICATION CAN MAKE.

31

OK! HERE'S THE DEAL! SEND ONE DOWN AND I'LL LET THE OTHER TWO GO!

FORGET IT, DOG!! WE'RE ALL IN THIS TOGETHER!! IT'S EITHER ALL OF US OR NONE!! SOLIDARITY TO THE END, GOT IT?!?

SOUNDED LIKE A GOOD IDEA TA ME, FLUFFY.

SURE. WHY NOT?

FLUFFY?

YES, CUDDLES.

I GOTTA GO REAL BAD.

RIP SHRED

TEAR REND RIP SHRED

YOU MIGHT WANNA HOLD IT.

FLUFFY?

YES, CUDDLES?

HOW LONG DO YOU THINK WE'LL BE UP HERE?

A LONG TIME CUDDLES. A LONG, LONG TIME.

34

41

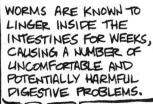

45

THEY'RE REAL PROFESSIONALS WHEN IT COMES TO THE SIMPLE THINGS.

SOME FOLKS LIKE TO LEAVE, THEIR ROMANCE TO FATE....

OR USE THOSE COMPUTERS, TO SEE HOW THEY RATE....

BUT I DON'T NEED GIMMICKS, TO LOOK UP MY MATE....

JUST GIMME A DOG PARK, TA FIND ME A DATE!

HE THINKS YOU GOT NICE—

WHAM! WHAM! WHAM! WHAM! WHAM! WHAM! WHAM!

WHAT'D I SAY?!

WILL YOU PLEEEASE LET ME DO THE TALKING.

57

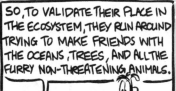

61

63

66

69

70

71

80

81

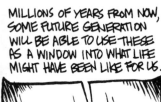

I'M NOT HERE TO ASK FOR ANYTHING.

I'VE BEEN PRETTY BAD THIS YEAR AND BOTH YOU AND I KNOW THAT I WON'T BE GETTING ANY PRESENTS.

IS THIS REAL?

SECURITY!!

ALL THE DRAPES ARE SHREDDED, SO I'LL NEED SOME OF THOSE... AND NEW CARPETING IN THE HALL WHERE HE TORE THAT HOLE.

AND CALL MRS. LAWRENCE'S LAWYER TO SEE IF SHE'LL SETTLE OUT OF COURT. I'D BE HAPPY TO PAY ALL OF HER MEDICAL BILLS.

SHE HAD THE RESTRAINING ORDER LAST YEAR. REMEMBER THAT?

WHERE DO YOU PEOPLE COME FROM?

93

94

108

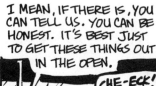

PING!

WHAT AN UNBELIEVABLE PERFORMANCE MEL HAS PUT ON FOR GOLF FANS TODAY!

HE IS ONLY ONE STROKE AWAY FROM CLINCHING THIS YEAR'S PISMO BEACH MILLION-DOLLAR PURSE...

...IF HE CAN JUST CLEAR THE WINDMILL.

HOLE THREE IS THE DREADED CASTLE KEEP! IT'S A PAR FIVE.

AIM FOR THE ASCENDING DRAWBRIDGE AND ANGLE YOUR BALL THROUGH THE CLOSING GATES.

BUT BEWARE! DON'T OVERSHOOT YOUR BALL INTO THE MOAT OR YOU'LL HAVE TO FACE THE FEROCIOUS MAN-EATING CROCODILES!

OOOHHHH... SCARY.

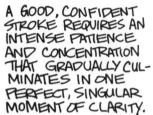

WELL, HELLO THERE LITTLE KITTY CAT!

SLASH!

I DON'T GET IT. EXPLAIN IT TO ME ONE MORE TIME.

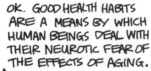

OK. GOOD HEALTH HABITS ARE A MEANS BY WHICH HUMAN BEINGS DEAL WITH THEIR NEUROTIC FEAR OF THE EFFECTS OF AGING.

BY EXERCISING REGULARLY, I CAN ADD UP TO TWENTY YEARS TO MY LIFE!

SO THAT'S TWENTY MORE YEARS YOU CAN SPEND IN NEUROTIC FEAR OF THE EFFECTS OF AGING.

EXACTLY.

FITNESS WORLD

BA-WANG BWANG B' SPANGNG - SPIN BA-DANG DING DI DING BWANG-GA-D DA BWAN BI

NICE GOIN'!

127